THE A-Z OF
POSITIVE THINKING

Dear Emma

Hope this
is useful

Amanda x x
x

Christmas 99

ABOUT THE AUTHOR

Neil James served in the Royal Fleet Auxiliary as an Engineer Officer before studying engineering at the University of Newcastle upon Tyne. His interest in motivation and continuous learning led him, in the summer of 1994, to co-found Quest Education & Development to further promote the Freedom Seminar, a process for personal development. He lives in South London.

THE A-Z OF POSITIVE THINKING

A New Vocabulary to Change Your Life

NEIL JAMES

Hodder & Stoughton

British Library Cataloguing in Publication Data
A record for this book is available from
the British Library

ISBN 0 340 73568 6

Printed and bound in Great Britain by St Edmundsbury Press

Hodder and Stoughton Ltd
A Division of Hodder Headline PLC
338 Euston Road
London NW1 3BH

With love to Teresa
A very special friend

The important issue
is not so much what we think we
want, but more a case of what we
want to think.

N. James

PREFACE

This book, like any project, started with a small seed of an idea. The eventual stimulus to write it all down and publish was a negative experience that, once antidoted and negated, turned into an outstanding opportunity for personal growth. They say that even something as beautiful as a pearl starts as a small piece of grit inside the oyster. That's how I now see that initial stimulating event: another bit of grit in life from which to learn, grow and further the path of love and life.

I know from personal experience, business and testimony from friends that all these strategies do work. As I say in my classes, if you like the ideas – great! Use them, work with them. If, on the other

hand, you don't see anything of value to you –
great! Just trash the idea and move on to another
that fits and feels right for you. There are no right
or wrong ways in growing. Growth happens
because we want it to happen.

Neil James
London
November 1998

ACKNOWLEDGMENTS

Arthur Koestler said in his book *The Act of Creation* that humour, much like creativity, comes from a sudden shift in our perception – a shift from one framework or perspective to another. In an instant a realisation reveals itself to us. Suddenly we see or think of everything differently.

I've always relished those slips, those sudden shifts in perspective. I say always, but that is not exactly true. Many of them I did not like at all at the time. Rather I grew to appreciate them, in much the same way as I now enjoy a mature single malt.

Acknowledgments are my maturing appreciations. This book is a consequence of many slips and shifts, of failures turned into successes. It could not have occurred without others being involved, without slips and bridges between personalities. The inspiration comes from others; from ideas distilled, crystallised, internalised, reformulated, shifted and moved.

I wish to acknowledge the writings of James Kavanaugh and in particular his poem, 'Will You Be My Friend', which helped me on my path. On this path I've received help, support and encouragement from the following: Caroline Rogers, Charlie Tveit, Ashley Wallman, Ilesh and Dushyant Patel and the many people that I've been fortunate enough to meet in my chosen profession.

Special tributes are owed to Tess Moore for her creative input, Isabel Losada my agent and Judith Longman my editor.

I am also deeply grateful to Teresa who in large measure was the catalyst and inspiration for bringing this book to print.

THE SEED OF AN IDEA

Have you ever wondered where all the negativity comes from? Why it is, with all that's great, good and beautiful, that we still seem to naturally gravitate back to those good old negs?

Well, it might have a lot to do with the fact that in an average-sized dictionary containing 31,460 words, there are only 1,705 that can be seen to be positive, strong, powerful and stimulating. That is just over 5 per cent of the words available to use. Moreover, there are over three times as many disempowering, sniping, griping, belittling and critical negative words. With 5,890 negatives to 1,705 positives, is it any wonder that the natural flows of conversation, thought and ideas are going to be strongly biased to the negative, especially when we seem to be able to roll the negatives off our tongues at a rate far in excess of three to one!

We are essentially our thoughts, and our language is going to be dramatically influenced by those thoughts. So if I have any goal in mind at all for this book, it is to reverse the trend for negative thinking, language and actions and to make a difference to the ways in which we use our minds in any given set of circumstances. As George Bernard Shaw was so fond of quoting,

'I don't believe in circumstances, for the people who get on in this world are the people who go on out and look for the circumstances they want and if they can't find them, they make them.'

So where did the idea for this book of positive words come from? What was the seed?

I was at a conference in York. As I walked past a group of our Swiss associates I overheard part of their conversation. 'The secret is you have to be **Living, Laughing and Learning**.' That was it; that was all. Just a snippet of a conversation. About what I have no idea, but as I walked past, it captured a piece of my mind and stayed there working away and growing. Now I'm a magpie for ideas. I carry a small notebook with me at all times, to jot down thoughts, impressions, quotes and ideas, and this little snippet went straight inside. It did more than that though. It continued to work at me and I found myself playing with the concept. **Living, Laughing and Learning**. Powerful, positive empowering words. Words of life.

When I returned from the conference I wrote the three words up on the dry-wipe board I have in my office and let the idea stay in limbo for a while. Like any true idea, it didn't just stay still.

This one started to grow, slowly at first, with the addition of just one word – **Loving**. I felt this was a stronger message, that this is what life is all about – **Living-Laughing-Loving-Learning** – and I adopted it as my motto.

Over the period of a month or so, three other letters appeared on my office board, attracting for a number of reasons their own words which were:

Fun-Free-Friends-Fame
Happy-Healthy-Horny-Holy
Energetic-Exciting-Enthusiastic-Extraordinary

I started trying them out. People would ask, 'How are you?' and I'd say right back, 'Well, I'm Happy, Healthy, Horny and Holy.' Some people would look at me as if I was totally crazy, but the majority would smile, and if I'd used the Es they would say, 'You certainly are extraordinary!'

The point though is that I was having fun with it and I noticed that other people's attitudes and mine shifted as a consequence. It sure beat that old litany of 'Oh, I'm all right, how are you?' or that old faithful 'Oh, not too bad today. My neck's playing up a bit. Pity it's so cold. How about you? Still got that trouble with your back?'

As with anything that works, you start to explore it a little more and so I started another notebook, indexed A–Z no less, and started jotting down all the good words I came across: Terrific, Exotic, Radiant, Enthralling, Sensational, Artistic, Alluring, Noble, Natural, Erotic, Tender, Unique, Real, Now, Enterprising, Remarkable, Inspiring, Spectacular, Beautiful and many more.

As the notebook slowly and gradually began to fill up, I started to notice a dramatic shift in my attitude to situations and people. An additional benefit which was to prove very useful later on was that by simply reading or speaking aloud the positive words, I was able to change my state of mind, my attitude, remarkably quickly.

ATTITUDES

There are times when a thought strikes you and you go 'Aha!/Eureka!' Probably one of the most graphic Ahas I ever had in my life was when I was reading a book by Viktor Frankl, *Man's Search for Meaning*. He was describing all kinds of horrors that we needn't go into here. In the midst of all this killing, death and torment, he came to the realisation and awareness of the greatest pearl of wisdom, in my opinion, yet uttered by a human being. This pearl is so powerful that I'll not hold back and disguise it or dilute it in any way. This truth simply states that:

'the ultimate freedom, the final freedom we have, that can never be taken away from

us, is the ability to choose our attitude in any given set of circumstances'.

Frankl saw individuals dividing into two types. There are those that give up hope: 'Woe is me, poor me. Why has this terrible thing happened to me? There is nothing I can do to help myself.' Others say to themselves: 'OK. I can accept this. I accept that this is awful, that I don't particularly enjoy this happening to me. But what can I do to improve on the matter? I'm going to get out of this jam. I'm going to do everything humanly possible to make the best of this situation by looking at what I can do personally. What is within my own power to influence, perhaps to change and rectify this situation?'

I imagine that if you're like me (human) you've probably come across examples of these attitudes either in your own experience or seen them in friends, relatives, colleagues and peers. There are those who acquiesce, abdicate and stop growing. And there are those who decide to take personal responsibility for their own thoughts and circumstances.

To show that there is nothing new in the world of ideas, when it comes to people's attitudes and behaviour, I'd like to draw on some wisdom from 2,500 years ago, from classical Greece. The scholar and philosopher Plato had many adages but the one that holds unbelievable currency today is that he believed, like Frankl, that people gravitate towards two zones, a zone of influence and a zone of concern. (See Figure 1.)

Now people who operate totally in their zone of concern are generally people who are out of control, who are continually moaning about this, that, or the other. We've all met them. You know

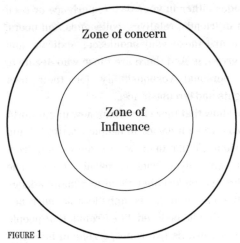

FIGURE 1

Zones of Influence and Concern

the conversations, 'Oh, why won't the government do...', 'If only the company would...', 'Typical, isn't it? Just look at the weather! Why it always does this I don't know.' You catch the message?

You see, people who operate away from their zone of influence are caught in a habit of looking continually outside of themselves for solutions. They adopt an external habit, and want others to make everything right with their world. Does that make sense? Of course it doesn't! It's not looking for solutions that are within their control.

So let's look at the other zone, the zone of influence, and see what a difference it makes. There always seem to be crises going on in the world. Famines, wars, ethnic cleansing, terrorism, despots... Now individually we probably have the attitude that there is not a heck of a lot we can do about any of them, outside of donating or perhaps even lobbying. We may be concerned but we probably do not have much influence at this precise point in time, right?

People who are what is termed 'well-centred' will recognise this. They may well be concerned, but say, 'Let's focus on what we can do to influence', or even more importantly, 'Let's grow ourselves, our zone, to start having an influence on those areas that we are concerned with.' For instance, I know a man who works for the Crown Agents. He was vitally concerned about the issues in Bosnia and so created a position for himself whereby he could have an influence, using all his skills in people management and logistics to make a difference. He ensured that the aid convoys got through to where they were needed. He grew his zone of influence to encompass part of his zone of concern.

That, in essence, is what a positive attitude is about: the ability to choose the attitude we want in a given set of circumstances and then to go out and do something about it. It doesn't have to be so graphic and serious. It could just be something simple, like something that happened to me, where an old school friend called up and said, 'We have not talked or seen each other in a while, and so I thought I'd do something about it.' Is that a positive, proactive action and attitude or what? So pick up that phone, write that letter, tell your partner how much you love them and what they mean to you, but more importantly, do it now. Be influential in your own world.

THOUGHTS

Another pearl of wisdom that sometimes helps to clarify which zone we are in is the well-known quote from Reinhold Niebuhr:

'Grant me the serenity to accept the things that I cannot change, the courage to change those that I can, and the wisdom to know the difference.'

The difference between those situations that you cannot change and those that you can change, the difference between our zone of concern and our zone of influence is only our attitude, and our attitude is dictated by our thoughts alone.

Let me give you a personal example. I was sitting down with Caroline, a friend of mine, a while back, having a great conversation and a coffee, when she said, 'NJ, do you really believe all this stuff you talk about, that no matter what happens you can control your thoughts and that this will make it all right?'

I said I did and gave her this example. 'I'm in this relationship with a wonderful woman, someone I think the world of, when at 8 p.m. one evening the phone rings. Now at 7:59 p.m. these are my exact thoughts and feelings about her: Hope, Love, Future, Joy, Togetherness, Adventure, Sensuality, Growth, Ecstasy, Friendship, Kindred Spirits, Closeness, Intimacy, Happiness, Respect, Delight, Faith, Warmth, Honesty, Desire, Power, Trust. Thoughts that she's very Special. A clear picture, right?

'Now, at precisely 8 p.m., just a few seconds after all these strong positive feelings and thoughts, as a consequence of one thing she said to me on the phone, my thoughts are: Gutted, Sick, Cold, Angry, Disappointed, Disbelieving, Disempowered, Hurt, Discarded, Jealous, Lost, Sad, Very sad, Betrayal, Fearful, Tearful, Poor Me, Why Me, Pessimistic, Bereft... A very different picture, agreed?

'But what had really changed, what had happened here? At one moment I was feeling on top of the world, positive and strong; at the next I'm feeling destroyed. Nothing physical had occurred, but mentally I had taken a message (and it could have been any message), internalised it and instantly, because of my attitude, I had changed my whole mentality. My whole attitude shifted from a positive frame to a negative one. I had changed myself in the way I'd reacted to the news.

'Now, did I stay there? Of course not, because I know the value of looking at my thoughts and my zones of influence. I know that in any given set of circumstances I have the freedom to choose my attitude. I would like to say that I'd reversed the whole scenario just as quickly, but I'm still learning and growing too. By 8:30 p.m. though, I had begun to grasp the elemental truths of what I needed to do. I began to think to myself, wait a minute here, let's look at this situation, if this is how I was feeling (Hope, Love, Joy, Friendship…) and this is how I'm feeling now (Angry, Hurt, Lost, Tearful…), which do I prefer? Well, there was no contest. The 7:59 list definitely made me feel more empowered.

'So I made the conscious decision to start the switch back to the positives because, let's be honest, what had really changed? I had been presented with a situation that was out of my immediate zone of influence. Somebody else (irrespective of how much I might love them) had made a decision that for them, at that precise moment in time, was right and important. The opportunity I had been presented with was to look at my own attitude, take responsibility for controlling my own thoughts and think: Serenity, Courage and Wisdom.

'Sure, I could have gone out and got blind drunk, like I always had in the past when confronted with such acutely emotional issues – but I didn't. Sure, I could have stayed angry, bitter, feeling sorry for myself and built up a portfolio of hate, jealousy, why me? and all that negative baggage – but I didn't. How constructive would those coping strategies have been? Instead I took control.

'I decided to see this situation as an opportunity to focus on the positives, on how I still really was feeling beneath all this anger. I used the thought antidotes continually to stay in a positive frame of mind. I listened to that still quiet voice deep within and I looked for a way forward.

'The results were quite dramatic. My whole demeanour changed very rapidly. I became very aware that I was in control. A few days later when we met, we had the most constructive, positive, loving time together we'd ever had. So yes, Caroline, I do believe that no matter what happens, we can control our thoughts.'

So, when somebody decides to pull our chain, when something unexpected occurs that knocks us away from our centre, let's look back to that centre, take charge and choose in Frankl's words, 'the attitude we want in any given situation'. Let's acknowledge our ultimate freedom: the freedom to choose and make the circumstances that we desire.

Positive Thinking

THE ANTIDOTES: HOW TO USE THEM

Albert Schweitzer said:

'People must cease attributing their problems to their environment and again learn to exercise their will, their personal responsibility.'

What are the antidotes? How do they help you to stay positive? They are an exercise in taking responsibility for what goes into our minds. They are a living list of words. They are positive, strong, vital words, words that evoke feelings of strength and control, words that raise positive emotions, words to aspire to, to move towards and words to whisper to our loved ones.

They may be words that you feel apply to you

or another. Perhaps if you're in love or in a relationship you may want to go through the list and highlight the ones that you feel are applicable to your lover. Remember though that when you do:

'What we see in others is invariably what we see within ourselves.'

So you cannot fail to give yourself a boost too. It's the ultimate win-win of a present: not only do you give but you also receive.

Another way of using the words is to dip in whenever a negative event, comment or thought comes winging its way towards you, like I just did a moment ago, when I realised there was a nagging doubt eating away at the edges of my consciousness.

It has been shown that it is impossible to hold two contrary thoughts in our mind at the same time. I can guarantee that if you've got a negative one and you look down through the antidotes, picking out the ones that speak to you, that negative thought will not stick around for long. It will very quickly ride out of town.

Another way of using them is to use what are known as 'present-tense sentence stems', attaching the antidotes. For example:

I am Happy, I am Trusting, I am Spectacular.
I am Brilliant, I am Free, I am Phenomenal...or
I have a Mentor, I have Love, I have Health.
I have a Bright Future, I have Good Friends...

The stems are a way of acknowledging who we are and what we really have going for us in our lives. Can you see that the antidotes then become completely personal to you and you alone? They can be used for positive affirmations, personal mottoes, goal-setting, vision and mission. Best of all, they are constantly and forever renewable; they are not a limited resource, something that can be taken away. Rest assured you cannot run out of them and they are always there for you. Your imagination is the only limitation.

So let's turn to these mysterious and positive words and let's go explore, looking for the words that may change your life or at the very least some of your perceptions.

Happy Antidoting and remember, you cannot overdose on positive thoughts.

THE JAMES PHARMACY INSTRUCTIONS

PLEASE READ CAREFULLY

Remember antidotes are for poisons and negative thoughts are the poisons of the mind. If you do not have the poison, you do not need the antidote. If you do, then take several hundred of them every day from the moment you awake to the instant you sleep.

WARNING

You may find some side effects which catch you unawares. One common consequence is that you may find yourself smiling and laughing uncontrollably at the strange negative antics of those around you who are not on the same medication, who are not antidoting. Do not be discouraged, you are sane.

These positive word capsules are very, very good for you. Keep taking the tablets.

THE ANTIDOTES

Ambitious, **Amazing**, **Adventurous**, **Achiever**, Ahead, Alive, Alert, Alluring, Adonis, Allowed, Allah, Amiable, Amicable, Amorous, Amused, Adored, Adroit, Anointed, Ardent, Artistic, Assertive, Astral, Atman, Attractive, Authentic, Able, Absorbed, Antidotal, Apollo, Awesome, Apostolic, Action, Acclaimed, Accomplished, Ace, Adonai, Alpha and Omega, Assured, Achieve, Active, Adept, Admired, Aphrodite, Aesthetic, Aspiring, Attitude, Animated, Agile, Angel, Ability, Ablaze, Athletic, Ascending

Bouncy, **Blissful, Brilliant, Beautiful,**
Balanced, Bearing, Beatific, Believe,
Beloved, Begin, Beneficent, Benefactor,
Benign, Benevolent, Be, Buddha, Blatant,
Broadminded, Bewitch, Blessed, Bold,
Bonny, Boss, Bountiful, Brainy, Bacchus,
Boyish, Brave, Brazen, Breathe, Butterfly,
Brahma, Bright, Ballistic, Ballsy, Boost,
Born, Bouncing, Balm

Centred, Creative, Colourful, Committed, Calm, Can, Candid, Champion, Change, Celebrate, Cerebral, Certain, Character, Cheeky, Caesar, Curious, Confident, Conscious, Control, Cool, Cosmopolitan, Cracker, Crazy, Cultivated, Compassionate, Competent, Composed, Conquering, Considerate, Constant, Constructive, Contemplative, Content, Classic, Czar, Christ, Clever, Cognisant, Comical, Commanding, Communicator, Courageous, Carpe diem, Clear, Capable, Capacity, Captivating, Care, Catholic, Chief, Chivalrous, Chuckle,

Creating, Commitment, Cleave, Cherish, Charged, Charity, Charm, Cock-a-hoop, Confucian, Caress, Cathartic, Certitude, Captivate, Composed, Congratulations, Cohere, Coherent, Coach, Conviviality, Creativity, Congruity, Congenial, Congruous, Charisma, Charismatic, Celestial, Caring

Deserving, Dynamic, Dancing, Desired, Deserve, Diagnose, Direct, Discover, Doctor, Draw, Duplicate, Deduce, Defend, Deliver, Demand, Deny, Differ, Diligent, Dominate, Delighted, Destined, Distinguished, Diamond, Dance, Dapper, Dashing, Delight, Decide, Dedicate, Decisive, Determined, Disciplined, Drive, Direction, Desire, Dream, Develop, Diversity, Diverse, Developing, Dalliance, Delicious, Design, Descant, Doughty, Dreamy, Devoted, Devotion

Energetic, Exciting, Enthusiastic, Extraordinary, Envisage, Equilibrate, Enfranchise, Equitable, Erotic, Escape, Efficacious, Effuse, Educe, Effect, Evolve, Ecstatic, Eclectic, Excited, Elegant, Elevate, Elucidate, Embody, Enable, Enamour, Enchant, Entice, Essential, Ethereal, Endow, Enhance, Enigma, Enormous, Ensure, Entertain, Enthral, Enthralling, Expect, Endure, Exotic, Extroverted, Enterprising, Eagle, Earnest, Easy-going, Eccentric, Entrance, Esteem, Exercise, Eager, Educate, Encourage, Experience, Excel, Enlighten, Empower,

Equal, Ebullient, Evolving, Encouragement,
Education, Equality, Embrace, Everlasting

Fun, Free, Friends, Fame, Funny,
Father, Female, Fabulous, Facilitator,
Facet, Face, Fair, Faithful, Famous, Fancy,
Fantastic, Featured, Fascinating,
Fashionable, Fast, Favoured, Favourite,
Fearless, Feasible, Felicitous, Felicity,
Focused, Faith, Find, Feel, Found,
Fortunate, Fiery, Foxy, Fellowship,
Feminine, Forerunner, Foresee, Foresight,
Forgive, Form, Formative, Formidable,
Forthright, Fortify, Fortitude, Fortuitous,
Fortune, **Feeling, Flourishing, Forgiving,
Freeing,** Fortunate, Forward, Founder,
Foster, Fountain, Fragrant, Frank,

Fraternal, Freelance, Freedom, Fresh, Friendly, Frugal, Fruitful, Fertile, Fervent, Festive, Fidelity, Fighter, Figurative, Finalist, Financial, Finder, Fine, Finesse, Figurative, Finisher, Firm, First, Fisherman, Flamboyant, Flora, Fulfilled, Fulfilment, Fundamental, Future, Fit, Fitting, Flair, Flattered, Flavour, Flexible, Fluent, Fluid, Flying, Focused, Forcible, Forceful, Foremost, Founding, Flow, Flowing, Fulgent, Fiancee, Friendship

Growing, **Glowing, Giving, Glittering,**
Great, Good, Gallant, Golden, Grandiose,
Guide, Guiding, Green, Guru, Galactic,
Gallant, Gambler, Gatherer, Gay, Gaiety,
Genuine, Giant, Gigantic, Giggle,
Gladiator, Glamorous, Graphic, Gleeful,
Gnostic, Go-ahead, Godly, Glad, Golden
Rule, Goluptious, Good Looking, Goodwill,
Goodly, Governor, Graced, Gracious,
Graduate, Grafter, Grand, Grateful,
Gregarious, Gorgeous, Generous, God,
Glorious, Genius, Genteel, Gentle,
Gumption, Gaia

Happy, **Healthy, Horny, Holy,** Handsome, Handy, Hardy, Headstrong, Ha-ha, Harmonious, Hearty, Healing, Heart, Heaven, Heed, Hegemony, Hegemonic, Helmsman, Helpful, Herald, Heroic, Herself, Heterodox, Hewer, High, High Spirited, High-flyer, Hermes, Hindu, Honest, Hustle, Halcyon, Hale, High-minded, Hilarious, Himself, Hip, Historic, Hit, Homeric, Honey, Honeyed, Honoured, Honourable, Hoot, Hopeful, Hospitable, Host, Huge, Humming, Human, Humane, Humanist, Humble, Humility, Humour, Humorous, Hunter, Hustle, Hygienic, Hearten, Harmony, Holistic

Inspiring, Intimate, Inquisitive, Irresistible, Improviser, Impulsive, Increasing, Illuminated, Illustrator, Illustrious, Imaginative, Immanent, Immanence, Immanuel, Impassioned, Impelled, Impressive, Impromptu, Improving, Insightful, Isis, Insistent, Instigator, Instructive, Instrumental, Intellectual, Intelligent, Intense, Intending, Invulnerable, Independent, Individual, Industrious, Infatuated, Infinite, Inflamed, Influential, Informed, Ingenious, Initiator, Innate, Innocent, Inquiring, Interesting, International, Interpretive, Intrepid, Intrigued, Invaluable,

Inventive, Investigator, Invigorating, Invincible, Inviting, Impart, Impartial, Interdependent, Impeccable, Imperative, Imperial, Impish, Imposing, Impossible, Indescribable, Indomitable, Independent, Immune, Imminent, Immense, Inspired, Inspirational, Initiative, Iconoclast, Idealist, Igneous, Imbued, Immaculate, Irrepressible, Immediate, Insatiable, Integrate, Integration, Integral

Jubilant, **Joyful, Jammy, Juicy,** Je Ne Sais Quoi, Jewel, Just, Jah, Jasmine, Jaunt, Jaunty, Jest, Jesting, Jester, Jewel, Jinks, Jocular, Jocund, Joke, Joking, Jesus, Jolly, Jollification, Jovial, Jubilance, Jubilation, Jubilee, Judicious, Jehovah, Joyous, Joy

Knowing, **Keen, Kissing, Kind,** Knack, Kudos, Knowledgeable, Karma, Kindly, Kindle, King, Kindred, Knight, Kaleidoscopic, Keeper, Krishna, Key, Kiss

Living, Laughing, Loving, Learning,
Laudable, Laureate, Leader, Lean,
Legend, Lucid, Luminous, Lord, Levity,
Luminary, Leitmotif, Liberal, License,
Life, Lifespring, Liked, Lion, Lissome,
Loquacious, Lucky, Luscious, Liberty,
Lateral, Lavish, Locus, Lode, Lofty,
Logical, Logos, Long-lived, Lyrical,
Luxuriant, Love, Light, Lusty, Listen,
Lively, Laconic, Lantern, Light,
Lascivious, Latent, Light-headed, Libra,
Light-hearted, Light-minded, Like minded,
Lifelong, Lift, Lifeblood, Lyrical, Lucid,
Luminous, Lusty

Motivated, Magical, Marvellous, Myself, Mastery, Mutual, Motion, Momentum, Mindful, Minded, Miracle, Miraculous, Mirror, Mirth, Mission, Mitigate, Mnemonic, Mobile, Moderate, Modern, Modest, Modifier, Momentous, Moral, More, Mother, Most, Male, Motor, Mountainous, Mover, Mystery, Mysterious, Mystical, Mythic, Mana, Manitou, Munificent, Muse, Music, Mutual, Memorable, Mentor, Merciful, Meritorious, Machiavellian, Maestro, Magic, Magisterial, Magnetic, Magnificent, Main, Majestic, Merry, Mesmeric, Messenger,

Multifaceted, Maker, Manful, Managerial,
Manic, Mannered, Marvel, Massive,
Master, Mature, Mercy, Maximalist,
Mediate, Mediator, Mellow, Melodic,
Metamorphosis, Mahatma, Mecca,
Meteoric, Motivated, Move, Meaning,
Manage, **Masterful,** Model, Magnanimous,
Methodical, Meticulous, Mohammed, Mien,
Might, Millionaire, Madonna

Natural, **Novel, Noble, Now,** Necessary, Neat, Navigator, Negotiate, Neophyte, Nerve, Nice, Nirvana, Noisy, Nonconformist, Notable, Nourish, Nourishing, Nurture, Nubile, Numen, Numinousness, Nature, Nectar, Nestle, Nimble, Nymph, Notice, Notional, Numerate

Original, Optimistic, Open-minded, Oneness, Objective, Obliging, Observing, Observant, Odyssey, Oedipus, Olympian, Omnipotent, Omniscient, Orgasm, Oneself, Opportune, Opportunity, Optimist, Optimism, Options, Opulent, Oracle, Orator, Ordained, Ordered, Organised, Osmotic, Outlandish, Outlook, Outspoken, Overt, Ownership, Opportunist, Obstinate, Organic, Orgasmic

Positive, **Powerful, Persistent, Passionate,** Prominent, Providence, Perfect, Performer, Permanent, Pace, Pacific, Paean, Pagan, Painter, Palatable, Panache, Par, Paragon, Paramount, Pantheism, Pan, Pardon, Par Excellence, Parity, Partake, Part, Participate, Participant, Partner, **Peaceful, Precious, Playful, Phenomenal,** Patient, Peace, Peak, Pearl, Penetrate, Pensive, Perceived, Perceptive, Perennial, Permeate, Permit, Perpetual, Persevere, Persist, Persistent, Person, Personable, Personify, Perspective, Perspicacious,

Perspicuous, Penetrating, Persuade, Persuasive, Pertinent, Pervasive, Pharos, Phenomenon, Philander, Philanthropist, Philosopher, Philosophical, Phlegmatic, Phoenix, Photographic, Photogenic, Physical, Pillar, Pilot, Pioneer, Pious, Piquant, Placate, Platonic, Plausible, Play, Please, Pleasure, Pleasurable, Plenitude, Plucky, Plus, Poignant, Point, Pointed, Poised, Polemic, Polished, Polite, Pomp, Ponder, Popular, Positive, Positivist, Possess, Possible, Possibility, Postulate, Potent, Potential, Pounce, Practice, Practical, Pragmatic, Praise,

Pray, Precognition, Preconceive, Predispose, Precede, Predisposition, Prefigure, Premeditation, Premonition, Prepossess, Presuppose, Polymath, Privileged, **Precious, Progressive, Professional, Profound,** Precedence, Precedent, Precipitate, Precise, Precocious, Precursor, Predecessor, Predict, Premeditate, Predominate, Prefer, Preference, Preferential, Premier, Prepared, Prescient, Present, Presence, Presentable, Preside, Press, Prestige, Presume, Prestigious, Presumption, Presumptive, Pretty, Prevail, Prevalent, Pride, Proud,

Primacy, Prime, Principal, Pristine, Private, Privy, Prized, Proceed, Process, Procure, Prod, Prodigy, Produce, Productive, Profess, Proficient, Profit, Progress, Project, Projection, Prominent, Promise, Promote, Prompt, Propensity, Prophet, Propitious, Propose, Prospect, Prosper, Protect, Protest, Proud, Prove, Provide, Prowess, Prudent, Psychic, Punctual, Pupil, Pure, Purify, Purpose, Pursuant, Push, Perfection, Providential

Quick, **Quiet, Questing, Quoted,** Qualify, Quality, Query, Question, Quicken, Quaker, Quiet, Quiescent, Quintessence, Quintessential, Quixotic, Quizzical

Radiant, Relaxed, Romantic, Rich, Resourceful, Responsible, Resolute, Respected, Reveal, Recognise, Relax, Relaxing, Raconteur, Racy, Radiance, Radiate, Radical, Rally, Randy, Rabbi, Revered, Rapt, Rapturous, Rate, Rational, Rationalise, Ray, Razzle, Readdress, Reaffirm, Rearrange, Reassert, Reassess, Refund, Rebuild, Recharge, Recommence, Reconsider, Reconstruct, Recover, Recreate, Redirect, Rediscover, Redistribute, Redress, Re-embark, Re-emerge, Reinforce, Re-establish, Refashion, Reform, Refuse, Reinvigorate, Relive, Remake, Remodel,

Reorganise, Revalue, Reach, Ready, Real, Realise, Reap, Reason, Reasonable, Reassure, Reassured, Rebound, Recall, Receive, Reciprocate, **Rejoicing, Resurgent, Ready, Rare,** Recognise, Recollect, Recommended, Recommend, Reconcile, Recuperate, Recusant, Redouble, Redress, Refine, Refined, Reflective, Reformer, Refresh, Regal, Regard, Reinforce, Rejoice, Relate, Relativist, Released, Relevant, Relief, Relieve, Relinquished, Relinquish, Relish, Remarkable, Remembered, Reminiscent, Renaissance, Renewed, Renowned, Repaired, Repeat, Replenished, Reputable,

Requested, Required, Rescued, Reservoir,
Resilient, Resistance, Resolute, Resolved,
Resonant, Resourceful, Respected,
Respectable, Resplendent, Responsive,
Responsible, Responsibility, Rested, Restful,
Restorative, Restrained, Restraint, Results,
Resurrected, Retentive, Retrieved,
Retrospective, Revelation, Revered,
Reverence, Revolutionary, Rhapsodical,
Rhetorical, Rhythm, Rhythmic, Right,
Righteous, Rigorous, Rising, Robust,
Romanticist, Rosy, Rounded, Rover, Royal,
Rubicon, Rugged, Running, Rushing

Singing, Smiling, Sparkling, **Supporting,** Stylish, Splendid, Sensual, Searching, Smile, Sincere, Slim, Self-help, Strong, Sacred, Sacrifice, Sacrosanct, Safe, Sagacious, Sage, Sailing, Saint, Saintly, Salient, Sally, Salubrious, Salutary, Salvation, Sanctify, Sanctuary, Sane, Spring, Seductive, Sanguine, Sartorial, Sanguineous, Satisfied, Saucy, Saturn, Sangfroid, Savoir-faire, Savoir-vivre, Scholar, Scholarly, Scholastic, Scientific, Scrumptious, Scrupulous, Sculpturesque, Searcher, Searching, Secluded, Secular, Secure, Sedate,

Seductive, Sedulous, See, Seeing, Seen, Selective, Self-control, Self-confident, Self-determined, Self-educated, Self-esteem, Self-realisation, Self-respect, Self-starter, Self-will, Self-willed, Sense, Sensible, Sensitive, Sensuous, Sentiment, Sentimental, Separate, Serene, Serious, Serve, Share, Sharing, Sharp, Shimmer, Shine, Shiny, Shipshape, Showman, Significant, Significance, Sikh, Silent, Silence, Simmering, Simple, **Sunny, Serene, Successful, Someone,** Singular, Skilful, Skilled, Sleek, Slender, Slick, Smashing, Smile, Smooth, Smoulder, Sociable, Social,

Socratic, Solace, Solutions, Solve, Somebody, Sonorous, Sophisticated, Sorry, Soul, Space, Spark, Speak, Special, Specific, Spectacle, Speculate, Speedy, Spellbinder, Spellbound, Spirit, Soul-mate, Spiritual, Splendid, Splendour, Spontaneous, Spring, Stable, Stand-up, Star, Start, Stature, Status, Steadfast, Steady, Steersman, Sterling, Still, Stimulating, Stoic, Stout, Straight, Strategist, Strength, Strenuous, Stretch, Stress, Stringent, Strong, Struggle, Study, Studious, Stupendous, Sturdy, Style, Stylish, Subdue, Sublime, Substance, Substantial, Subtle, Succeed,

Success, Succinct, Succour, Succulent, Sufficient, Suffuse, Suggest, Suitable, Sumptuous, Super, Superb, Superfine, Superhuman, Superintend, Superior, Superlative, Superman, Supernatural, Supervise, Supple, Support, Striking, **Spectacular, Sensational, Sensual, Sunny,** Supportive, Supreme, Sure, Sunshine, Surprise, Survive, Survey, Sustain, Sweet, Sweetheart, Sweety, Swell, Swift, Swim, Swing, Swot, Sylph, Siva, Sympathy, Sympathetic, Synchronise, Synoptic, Synthesise, Systematic, Synergy, Synthesis, Surprising, Sexy

Talented, Tasty, Terrific, Trusting, Tasteful, Tempestuous, Tempting, Tender, Tacit, Taciturn, Tact, Tactical, Tactile, Taking-off, Talkative, Tall, Tally, Tangible, Target, Targeted, Taste, Teach, Teacher, Teamster, Technical, Technique, Teem, Teetotal, Teleological, Temperate, Tempestuous, Tenacious, Tenacity, Theatrical, Therapeutic, Thin, Thinking, Thinker, Thorough, Thoughtful, Thread, Threshold, Thrilled, Thrusting, Ticking, Tidy, Timeless, Timely, Tireless, Titillator, Titillating, Toast, Together, Tolerant, Tops, Topical, Torrid, Total, Touching, Tough,

Toward, Tower, Track, Traditional, Trainer, Tranquil, Transcend, Transcendental, Transfigured, Transformed, Transit, Transition, Translator, Transmit, Transpire, Transpiration, Transported, **Thrilling, Thankful, Treasured, True,** Travail, Travel, Traveller, Treasure, Treat, Tremendous, Triad, Tribute, Trim, Triumph, Triumphant, True-Love, Truism, Truly, Trust, Truth, Truthful, Try, Trying, Tuition, Tune, Turning Point, Tutor, Tutelage, Twinkle, Tumultuous, Tickle, Tickling

Undeniable, Unequalled, Useful, Unique, Utopia, Utopian, Unquenchable, Unrivalled, Unpredicted, Unprecedented, Unmatched, Unerring, Unearthly, Unpressured, Unperturbed, Unpretentious, Unrestrained, Upright, Urgent, Unorthodox, Unity

Vivacious, **Vigilant, Vivid, Virile,**
Vigorous, Venus, Valiant, Valuable,
Vegetarian, Verbal, Veritable, Vibrate,
Victor, Victory, Victorious, Vishnu,
Virtuous, Vocal, Vogue, Volatile, Voyager,
Visualise, Values, Vibrant, Vital, Vitality

Wonderful, **Warm, Wealthy, Wild,**
Well, Worthy, Wise, Wakeful, Watchful,
Wanton, Weird, Wholesome, Wide,
Wicked, Woo, Work, Worldly, Worship,
Worthwhile, Whole, Wilful, Willing,
Winner, Winning, Witty, Within-Without,
Wondrous

e**X**celling, e**X**citing, e**X**pecting,
e**X**ploring, eXtraordinary, eXtravagant,
eXuberant, eXultant, eXtrovert, eXtra,
eXtra Special, eXperiment, eXperimental,
eXplain, eXplore, eXpress, eXpressive,
eXquisite, eXternalise, eXtol, eXcellent,
eXcite, eXcuse others, eXercise, eXert,
eXhort, eXpect, eXpedite, eXperience,
eXpectation

Young, Yearning, Yours, Yes, Youthful, Yahweh, Yes to Life

Zippy, Zealous, Zestful, Zeus, Zeitgeist, Zonal, Zoroastrian

So Why Bother?

I'd imagine that, like many people I've talked to as a consequence of their reading this book, in places you've smiled and in places you've frowned. Some of it's for you and some of it's not. That's OK by me, because it's the smiles I'm looking for and anything that can be done to reverse that statistic of three times the negativity is pretty wonderful stuff.

The question was asked though, why bother? That's a good question on many different fronts. James Allen in his essay 'As a Man Thinketh' says:

It is not what we want but what we are'
and *'A man is literally what he thinks,*

*his character being the complete sum of
all his thoughts.'*

Marcus Aurelius wrote:

*'We become as our thoughts are usually
and habitually.'*

I've included a quote already:

*'The important issue is not so much what
we think we want, but more a case of
what we want to think.'*

The core theme is that without control over our
thoughts, what chance is there for our dreams?
And that's a vitally important issue to bother
with, wouldn't you say?

Let's analyse the above quote, *'It's not so
much what we think we want.'* Let's ask
ourselves the question, what is it that we think
we want? Ask it again and again, write down the

answers. Then ask the question, what thoughts do we have associated with these wants? Quite often what I find in working with individuals and groups is that the thoughts that they are having are incongruous with what they want.

For example, somebody thinks to themselves that they want peace, affiliation, career, wealth, friendship, success, acknowledgment, intimacy, etc. Yet the actual thoughts they associate with these wants are things like anger, frustration, unworthiness, fright, fear, anxiety, reluctance to give up status quo or perceived stability. It becomes apparent why the actual road towards those wants is slow going, if at all feasible.

No, it's the second part of the quote that has the real payback, *'It's a case of what we want to think, that's important.'* Try it. Look again at the things that you think you want and now think of the thoughts that would be essential and congruous in allowing those things to happen. What thoughts are necessary to put you back on the path to your dreams? I'd be willing to bet a million that they need to be positive, not negative. Now we realise that we have to control them continuously to stay in harmony with everything we want from life.

To get everything good and beautiful out of life we have to know what we want to think. This truism cannot be emphasised enough. We are literally the sum total of our thoughts. The last freedom that we have is the ability to choose the attitude we want in any given circumstances. The people who get on in this world are the people who go out and look for the circumstances they want and if they can't find them, they make them. Well-centred people realise that they have to stay where they can make a difference, instead of having pity parties about things outside their zone, about concerns they have no influence over.

We are our thoughts, and that realisation is a challenging issue for some people to accept. It can also be a courageous, serene and wise decision to accept it. Indeed, acceptance is a positive step, and positive steps are associated with positive thoughts.

You have here 1,705 helpful positive steps.

the Freedom Process

Socrates' famous dictum, 'First Know Thyself' is as relevant today as ever. On the following pages, *Freedom* is used as a step-by-step framework in helping us to find our own unique, independent and individual purposes. It is a process of finding what we want from life and a useful, positive first step on the path to truly knowing ourselves.

Freedom occurs when many interrelated events happen simultaneously. By working on different areas of someone's life, a certain synergy commences which helps move them along their path. It is a continuous and creative endeavour.

The best way to use the action points is to

look at each principle as a stepping-stone question. What do I want to focus on? What fears are hindering me right now? Where do I need to take responsibility? How can I gain more energy? What am I enthusiastic about? What disciplines would empower me?

Note that this is just a first step, but as the ancient sage Lao Tzu said,

'Even a thousand-mile journey starts with a single step.'

Make masses of notes. Be positive. Let's start our journey now.

FREEDOM

'No person is truly free, who is not Master of themselves'

EPICTETUS

Step 1: Fearlessness and Focus

Do you allow the fear of change and a lack of direction to dissipate your focus? Personal freedom comes from discovering your real purpose.

■ What do I need to Focus on right now?

■ Stay in the present moment. Focus on what *you* want to think.

■ What Feelings and Fears do I need to face up to?

fReedom

'People must cease attributing their problems to their environment and again learn to exercise their will, their own personal responsibility'

ALBERT SCHWEITZER

Step 2: Roles and Responsibility

How do you respond to choices? Do you procrastinate or seize the moment? Are you aware that your relationship with yourself is your responsibility alone?

■ Where do I need to take Responsibility?

■ What do I want to see happen in my Relationships?

■ Reach Decisions about what you are going to do. What is your Role going to be?

frEedom

'The greatest discovery of my generation is that human beings can alter their lives by altering their attitudes of mind'

WILLIAM JAMES

Step 3: Esteem and Experience

How much faith do you truly have in yourself and your abilities? Do you visualise success to develop even more confidence? Do you nurture a sense of self-efficacy?

- When was the last time you Exercised your Mind?

- Do you examine your Experiences and notice where your Self-Esteem comes from?

- Enlightenment will come with all those Ahas. Write them all down.

freEdom

'Our bodies are our gardens, Our wills are the gardeners'

WILLIAM SHAKESPEARE

Step 4: Energy and Enthusiasm

Have you ever assessed the cost that negative thoughts and people can have? Discover the control you can develop with an attitude that will sustain you.

- When did you last Exercise your Body?

- Do you Encourage Enthusiasm in all you do and with all the people you meet?

- Energy makes the difference. (Find it. Harness it. Use it.)

FreeDom

'Knowing what to do isn't enough unless you have the self-discipline to do it'

HARVEY McKAY

Step 5: Decisions and Detachment

Do you get anxious and uncertain about making major decisions? Find the secret of relishing uncertainty and reduce your anxiety in times of stress.

- What Decisions do I need to make?

- What Directions have I ever wanted to explore?

- Do you recognise that Detachment and Disassociation can lead to Freedom?

- What do I need to Detach from?

FREEDOM

'Life is an opportunity. *Take it'*
                        CHINESE PROVERB

Step 6: Options and Opportunity

Have you ever rejected or not seen opportunities that were available? Look for the options that are there for you and that will allow you to rise above the negative attitudes of others.

■ What Obstacles do I have to Optimistically Overcome?

■ Do I have an Open-minded attitude to developing myself?

■ How can Others help me to learn and improve?

FREEDOM

'The greatest motivator *of all is Love. Love what you do and Love who you are.'*

Step 7: Meaning and Motivation

Have you ever wondered why you do what you do, what the point of it all is? Learn to live with passion, inspiration, real commitment and sustainable *motivation*.

■ Where does my Motivation come from?

■ When do I have inner Motivation? Power comes from within.

■ Do I recognise that being Myself is the most empowering strategy I can adopt?

■ Have I realised that Mastery comes from Moving ahead now, with Meaning?

If we always think what we have always thought, we will always be what we have always been.

N. James

THE FREEDOM SEMINAR

If you would like more information about the Freedom Process please write to:

Quest Education & Development
PO Box 4702
London SW17 7QE

BOOKS TO INSPIRE

As a Man Thinketh, James Allen

Jonathan Livingstone Seagull, Richard Bach

The Power of Myth, Joseph Campbell

How To Win Friends and Influence People,
  Dale Carnegie

Encyclopaedia Britannica

Man's Search For Meaning, Viktor Frankl

The Fear of Freedom, Erich Fromm

The Common Denominator of Success, Albert Gray

The Tao of Pooh, Benjamin Hof

Think and Grow Rich, Napoleon Hill

Get a Message to Garcia, Elbert Hubberd

Search, James Kavanaugh

Will You Be My Friend, James Kavanaugh

The Act of Creation, Arthur Koestler

If You Meet the Buddha on the Road, Kill Him!,
  Sheldon Kopp

Effective Problem Solving, Martin Levine

Managing Yourself, Jagdish Parikh

The Road Less Travelled, M. Scott Peck

The Man who Mistook his Wife for a Hat,
  Oliver Sacks

The Alexander Technique, Chris Stevens

The Way of Life, Lao Tzu, trans. Witter Bynner

See You at the Top, Zig Ziglar